Luck the Duck

By Stephanie Bunt

Bunt Early Specialized Teaching

BEST
Books

Short "u" Vowel Sound Practice

This book was created using the B.E.S.T. method.

Before reading this book with your early reader, practice reading these words. First, read them to your early reader while pointing to the sounds each word makes. Then, have your early reader try. Point to each sound as he/she is reading the words and say the sounds to him/her, as needed. Begin reading the story once your early reader feels comfortable with these words.

When reading the story, read to your early reader a few times. As you are reading, point to the sounds/words you are reading. Now, have your early reader read. Point to the sounds/words as he/she is reading and say the sounds with him/her, as needed. Happy reading!

==You can cut out these focus words at the end of the book.==

<u>First</u>, practice these words.

Luck, duck, yuck, stuck, truck, lump, clump, jump, dump, bump

Once these words are mastered, go onto the next set of words.

of, the, pup, mud, dub, rub, tub, scrub, from, fun, sun, run, but, what, brush

Once these words are mastered, review the first set and go onto the next set of words.

sunk, spunk, stunk, junk, funk, trunk, chunk, dunks, defunct,

After practicing these words, review all the words.

<u>Now</u>, it's time to read the book, yay!

The definitions of some of these words are in the back of the book.
Explaining these words will help your child understand them.

"Luck the Duck" not only focuses on the short vowel U sound, but is also about a silly duck that is very curious and jumps into something smelly and as he tries different things to get rid of the smell, he just seems to get even dirtier. Finally, he goes into a tub and washes everything off. This book teaches us in an entertaining way that if we keep trying to reach our goal, even if it seems like it is getting worse, we should never give up because eventually we will figure out a way to solve our problem.

I want to thank my mom, grandparents, and the rest of my family and friends for continually loving and enabling me to become the person I am today. They allowed me to grow, flourish and bring my gifts into this world to then help others.
-Stephanie

Luck is a duck.

Luck runs into
a trunk of junk
that stunk.

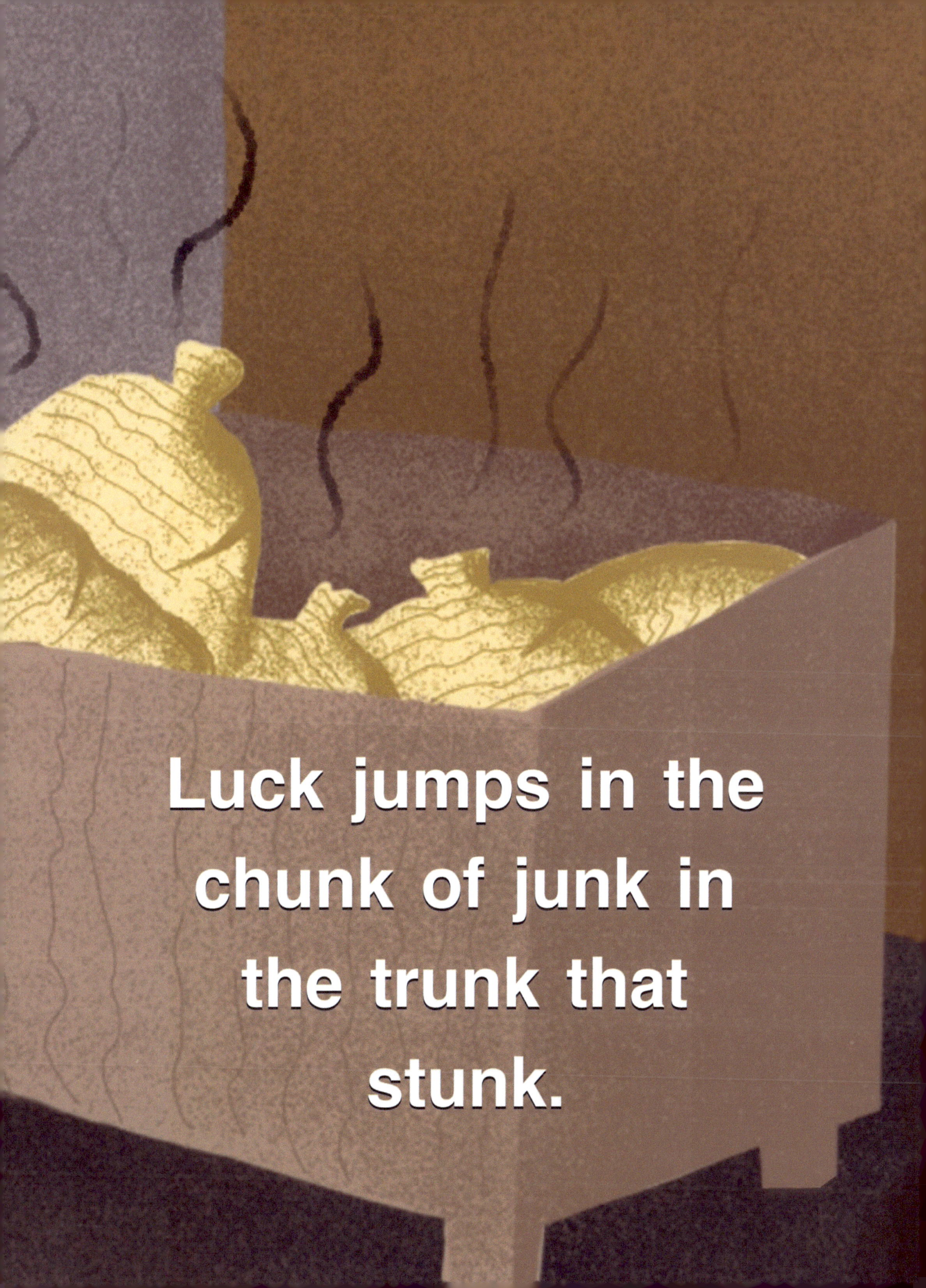

Luck jumps in the chunk of junk in the trunk that stunk.

Yuck, Luck stunk!

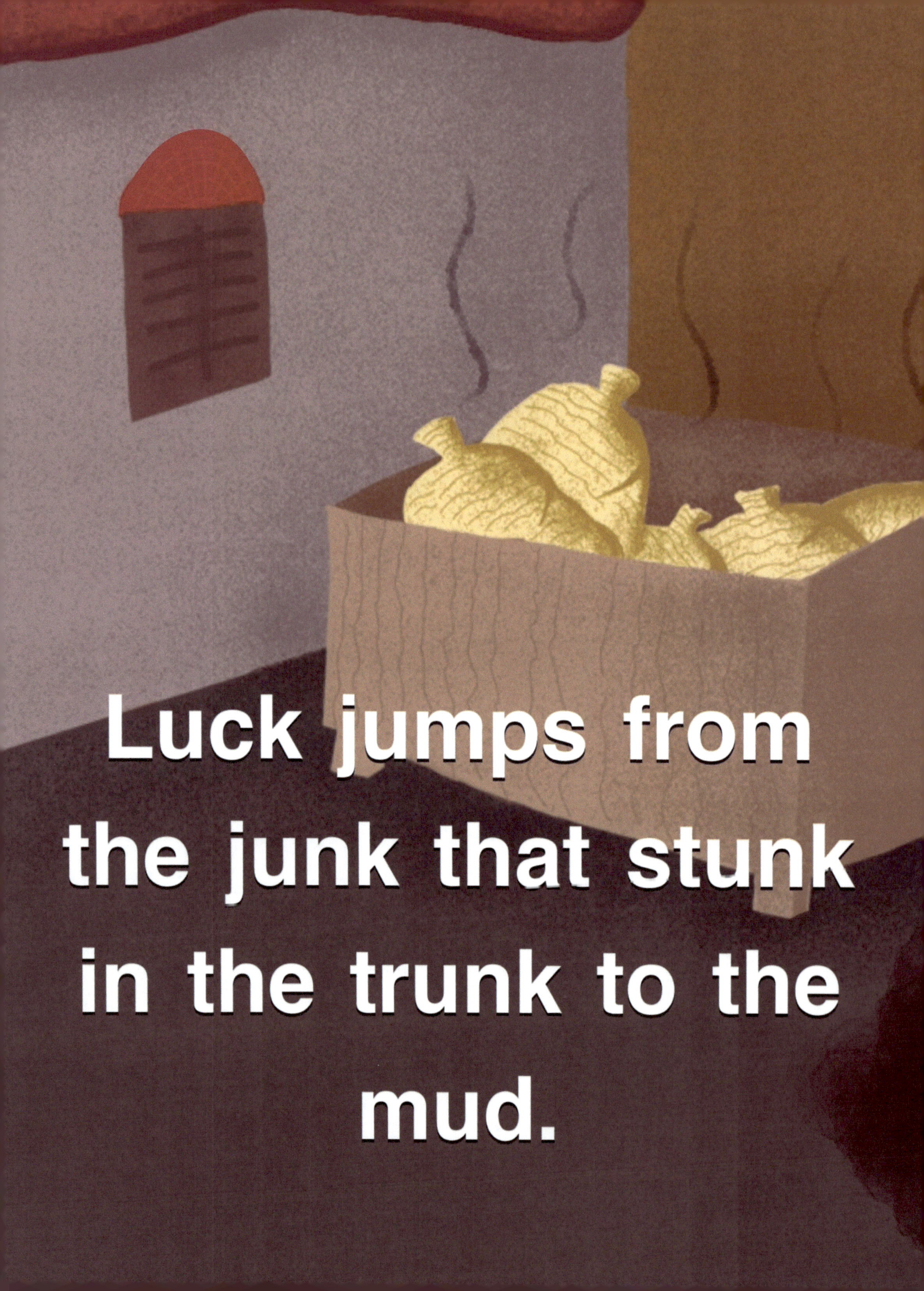

Luck jumps from the junk that stunk in the trunk to the mud.

Luck scrubs mud to brush what stunk from Luck. Luck rubs and scrubs the chunks of mud.

Luck rubs chunks of mud, but Luck stunk. Yuck!

A pup and truck bump in the mud. Luck lumps a clump of mud and jumps with a pup in the mud.

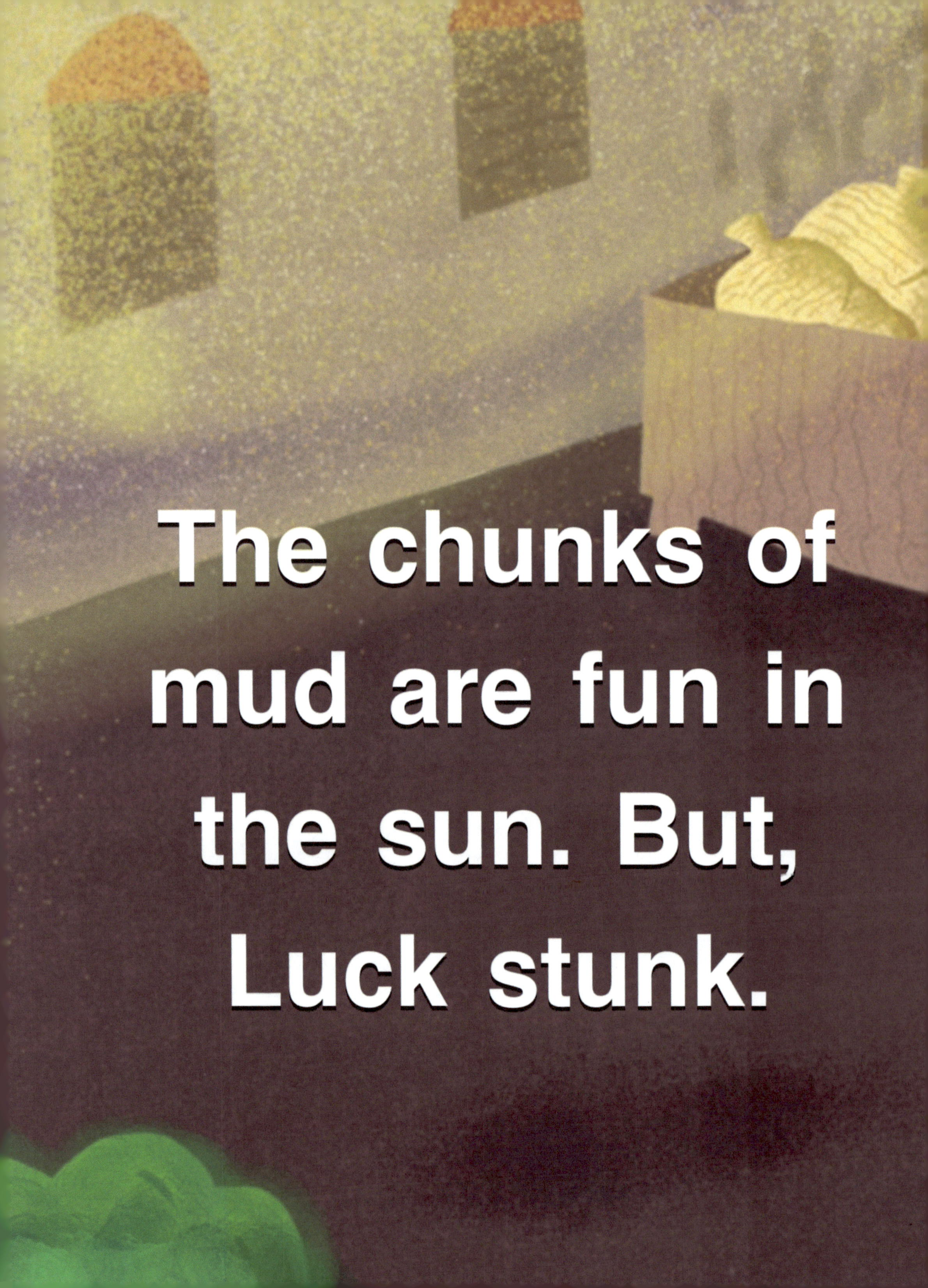

The chunks of mud are fun in the sun. But, Luck stunk.

Luck dunks a truck in the mud. The truck is a dump and sunk in the mud.

Luck, Pup, and the truck must be dumped in the tub.

Scrub a dub dub,
Luck dumps the
truck in the tub.

Luck and Pup
jump in the tub.

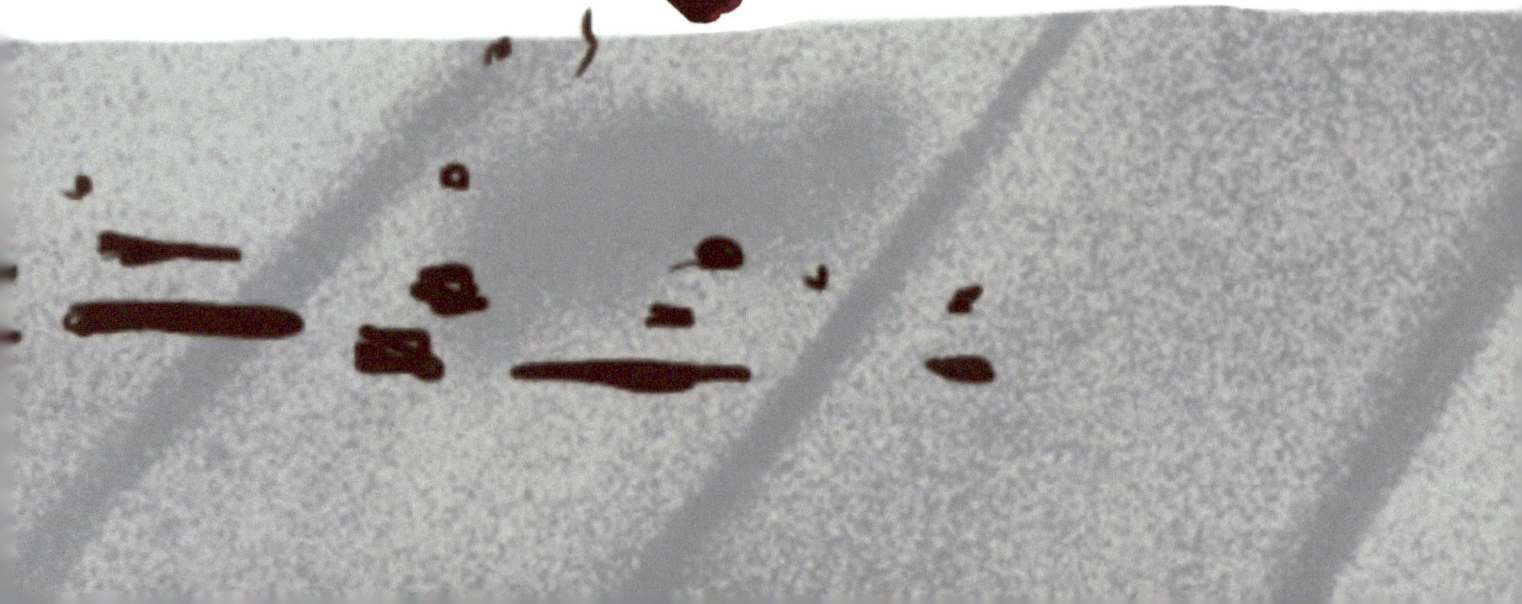

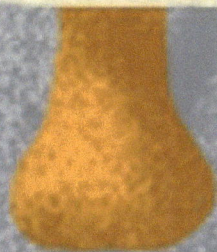

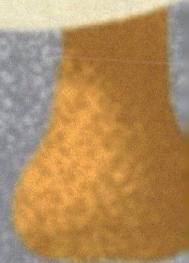

Luck and Pup rub and scrub in the tub.

Luck and Pup jump
and jump in the tub.
What a fun tub, Luck!

The funk that stunk and mud is defunct!

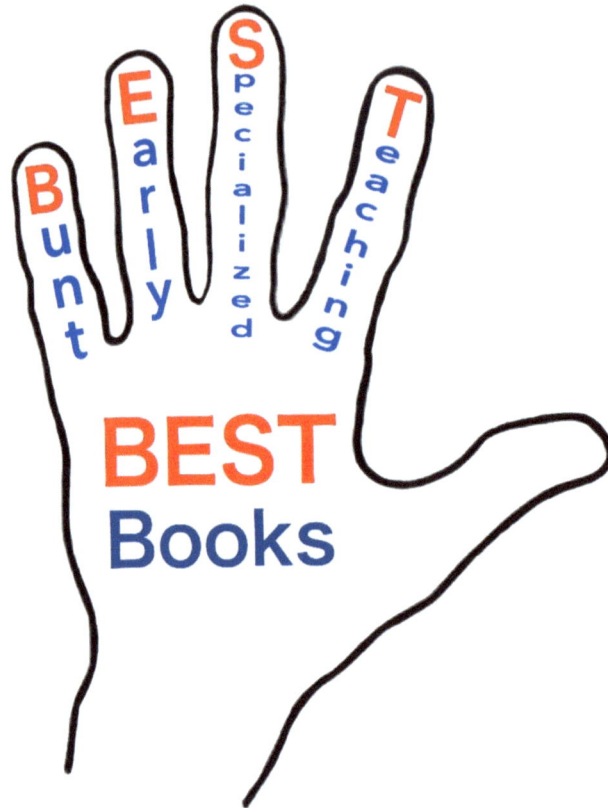

Bunt Early Specialized Teaching

Explain these words to your child for a better understanding of the book.

Definitions

Chunk: A thick piece of something.

Clump: To push something together or a compacted mass or lump of something.

Defunct: No longer exists/is there.

Dump: A place for depositing garbage.

Dunk: To fully dip something in a liquid.

Funk: An odd smell.

Lump: Push together/combine.

Scrub: To rub (someone or something) hard.

Spunk: To have spirit, confidence, feel great.

Stunk: To have had a bad smell.

Sunk: To have gone below the surface.

For extra practice cut out these words and read them.

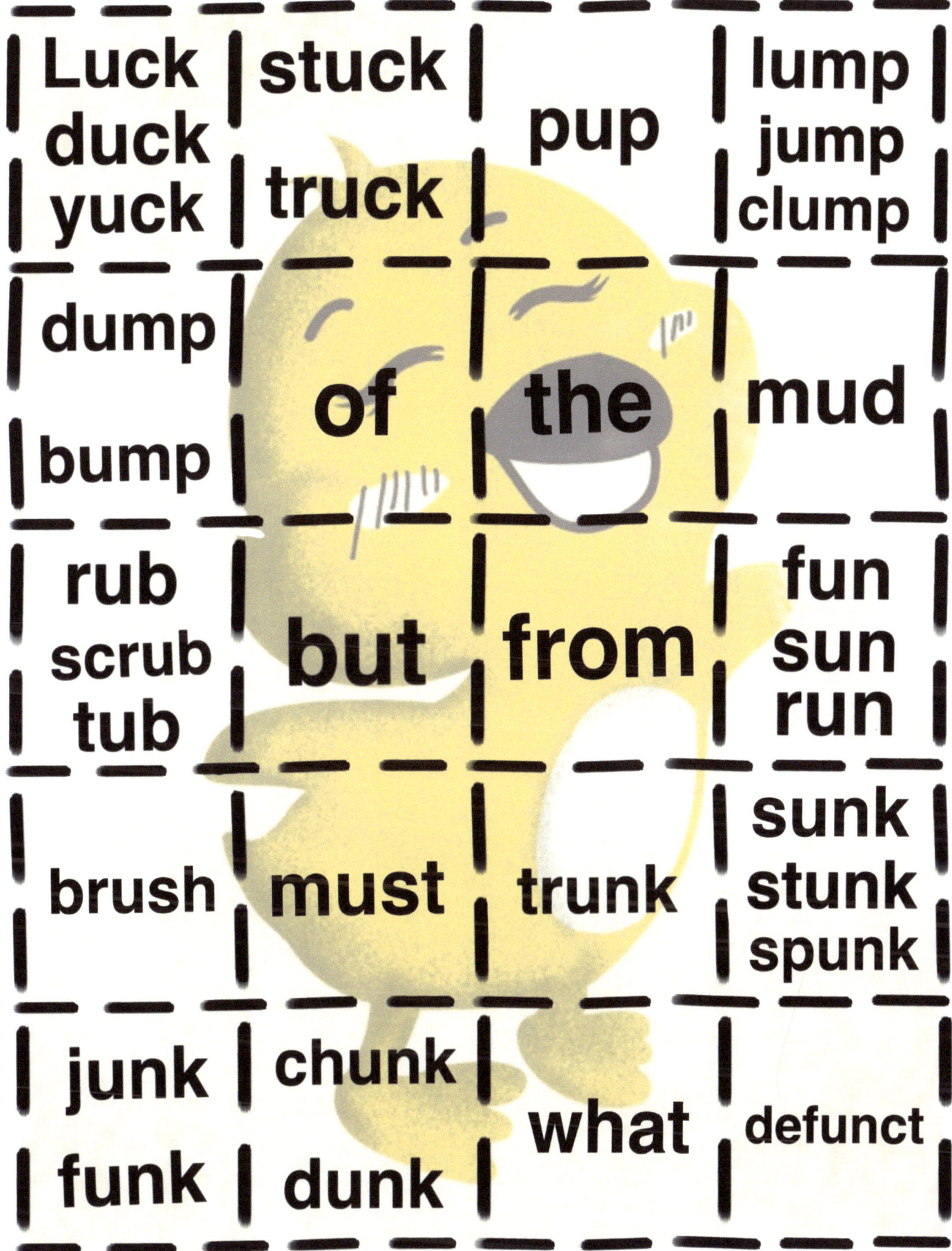

Luck
duck
yuck

stuck

pup

truck

lump
jump
clump

dump

bump

of

the

mud

rub
scrub
tub

but

from

fun
sun
run

brush

must

trunk

sunk
stunk
spunk

junk

funk

chunk

dunk

what

defunct